In the Buddha's Light

In the Buddha's Light

Photographs by Jack Parsons
Essay by Joanna Hurley
with a foreword by Joan Halifax

We dedicate this book to our beloveds,
Rebecca Parsons (1939-2019)
and William deBuys

Detail, wall, Luang Prabang

Photographer's Note

When I first went to Luang Prabang in 2007, with my wife, Rebecca, we felt immediately at home. The sweet lilt of the language, the inescapable beauty of the ever-present textiles, the human scale to the buildings, and the gentle flow of the two rivers, the Mekong and the Nam Khan, created an environment that we embraced, that kind of rare place that stays gently in your memory forever.

Several years later I returned to Lao with a good friend, Joanna Hurley, to do this project. I had thought a lot about Luang Prabang over that time, and my thoughts kept circling back to the temples (*wats*) and the lasting impression they had made. For me they were a visual reflection of the Lao people, and I was hoping that by visiting and photographing all thirty or so of those within and surrounding the city I would gain some small insight into the Lao world. In viewing the wats through my camera, watching the monks working, praying, even sleeping, the temples became an extension of them, and the buildings themselves magical reflections of their Buddhist world and culture. Somber and garish, small and large, modest and pretentious—it was all there, an exquisite harmony of color and light and a sense of design that spoke to me of the Lao people's ability to intuitively make beauty a constant in their lives. Of course there was always the interplay of poverty and wealth, of ignorance and knowledge, but the world that greeted me each day as we drove from temple to temple was one of profound beauty and peace.

JACK PARSONS

Publisher's Preface

THE INTERNATIONAL FOLK ART MARKET is an organization committed to the sustainability of global cultural traditions by presenting and honoring the artistic production of the peoples of the world. Every year, for the last 16, we have held a weekend Market in Santa Fe, New Mexico, that attracts over 150 artists from 50 countries to our city. Here they display their work and participate in a myriad of activities that showcase and disseminate the cultural diversity of the people of our planet. Our events include the weekend Market, artist trainings, musical performances, and an artists' procession on our central Plaza, where thousands of members of our community welcome the artists to our town.

We are pleased to participate in the publication of this beautifully written and illustrated book, which helps us to fulfill our mission of changing the world by preserving and supporting indigenous art and culture, of which the artistic and spiritual heritage of the peoples of Laos are powerful examples. We are pleased to share these living traditions with the world through the beautiful photographs of Jack Parsons, the moving and evocative essay by Joanna Hurley, and the heartfelt introduction by Roshi Joan Halifax of Santa Fe's own Upaya Zen Center.

As you page through this book, you will long for the landscape, temples, people and culture of Laos. We know you will find it inspiring.

STUART A. ASHMAN

Chief Executive Officer, International Folk Art Market

In the Buddha's Light

Monks on morning alms walk, Sisavangvong Avenue

Introduction

JOAN HALIFAX

THE FIRST MORNING IN LUANG PRABANG, Laos, at dawn, I saw them . . . the young, orange-robed monks drifting down the road in the pale early light. I remembered that more ordnance was dumped into this tiny country than any other location in the world—ever.

I recall thinking, "How can this be? What have we done? Why have we done this? It's not like these bombs are going to go away!" And that I could not come to terms with the idea of this atrocity. I couldn't then, and I can't now, so I turned my mind to the monks holding their begging bowls, moving silently from house to house, from street corner to street corner. Some of them looked like farm boys just out of the rice fields, others like they had just left their mother's house. A few had a very educated feel to them. On they walked, pausing to receive food, then offering a quietly chanted sutra, then moving along, eyes cast down, often with a subtle smile dancing across the lips.

The peace on the faces of the monks doing *bintabot,* or morning alms, did not betray a history of violence. Nor do the exquisite temples that can be found all over beautiful Luang Prabang, a city that hangs on the edge of the mighty Mekong River.

The Mekong, which is the beating heart of Luang Prabang, threads 2703 miles through China, Myanmar, Laos, Thailand, Cambodia, and Vietnam, finally finding her way through a web of deltas in Vietnam, and expressing her waters into the South China Sea. Mekong (*Mènam Khong* in Lao) can mean "Mother of Waters." And she is that, fertile, wild, and connective. I am in awe of the Mekong. I heard so much about this great river during the war in Vietnam, but until my visit to Laos, I had no idea how magnificent she was. I could see why Luang Prabang has thrived on her banks, and how she feeds the holy city literally and figuratively. And heals it.

I also could feel that Luang Prabang has long been the sacred center of Laos, the place where Lao spirituality is visible everywhere. In my time there, I discovered royal libraries, glittering shrines, small chapels, and exquisite temples filled with Buddha statues, both new and old, often donated by the faithful.

Buddhism has flourished in Laos for over a thousand years, having taken root in the thirteenth and fourteenth centuries. Wars, politics, and tribal affiliations have not driven out the Buddhism that is woven deep into the country's life and culture and whose presence is concentrated in the remarkable city of Luang Prabang. About fifty-three percent of the ethnic or lowland Lao people are Theravada Buddhist, which was introduced into this region in the eighth century by Mon Buddhist monks. The rest of the population are members of the forty-eight ethnic minorities, and they tend to practice their own versions of folk religions.

Incredibly, there are about 5000 Buddhist temples throughout Laos, a country comprising fewer than 100,000 square miles. Thirty-four of those temples are in in Luang Prabang. The temples are served by monks. Most Buddhist men in Laos become monks, even if only for a short period of time. Thus the drifting line of men who thread their way barefoot through the streets of the holy city in the early morning mists that rise off the Mekong and that float along with the monks as they move through the neighborhoods most of them know well.

What is Buddhism? And how is this tradition reflected in the temples in Luang Prabang? Buddhism is the fourth largest religion in the world, originating in India 2,500 years ago. Buddhism acknowledges the truth of suffering, its source, and that there is a path to transform suffering, and attain liberation from suffering. The path out of suffering entails living a life that is dedicated to non-harming, training the mind through meditation practices, and actualizing wisdom through realizing the truth that there is no inherent self of any being or thing.

Buddhism in Laos has its roots in the Theravada tradition (The Doctrine of the Elders), the earliest form of Buddhism, whose precepts are collected in the Pali Canon. Buddhism spread to Sri Lanka from India in the second century B.C.E., and monks, scholars, and missionaries made their way from there to Southeast Asia, where the teachings were eagerly accepted.

The temples of Luang Prabang reflect literally and figuratively the heart of Buddhism, which is a religion of transformation. The rooflines of temples soar into space. The facades of temples glitter with light. The interiors of temples are plain or highly adorned but always have a *rupa* (sometimes many), which is a statue of the Buddha, who exemplifies the spirit of awakening, or what it is to be a full and true human being.

Often, there are depictions of the life of the Buddha, painted, carved, or created out of beautiful glass mosaics that show images of the birth and enlightenment of the Buddha, as well as his death. I also visited some temples that looked a bit like discos, with gaudy lights shining on the altar. And other temples were illumined only by sunlight in the day and candles in the early morning and evening. Buddhism does not seem to discriminate when it comes to light.

Often marking the sacred boundary of temples are stupas, or small shrines containing relics that signal to worshippers and practitioners that they are on sacred ground. And gold is everywhere, gleaming gold, precious and cherished gold, letting practitioners know how rare is the gift of awakening.

This book brings to us the many deep and priceless treasures of this ancient city. The photographs capture faithfully the beauty of her temples and the humility of her monks. We are invited to enter these sacred spaces quietly and to take time to stop and see who we really are. The book itself is a meditation on light and shadow, a contemplation of one's inner life, a life that is mirrored by the beauty of these ancient shrines to awakening and those who tend them. We see through the eyes of the photographer a world of expressed potentialities. And through the words of the writer, we are introduced to the history, atmosphere, architecture, and friends of this remarkable place. Like the writer, we feel drawn to meditate as we turn the pages of the book.

As did both the writer and photographer, one morning, early, I got into a rickety boat on the Mekong and was taken to the two caves at Pak Ou. I was stunned by what I saw: thousands of Buddha statues of every size, tucked into large and small niches in the bowels of this labyrinthian cave complex. Colored lights illumined some of the largest statues, which were ablaze in garish green or red. Not infrequently, I found myself crawling carefully along walls to photograph these amazing icons. Finally I had to stop and just gaze at the wild and uncanny beauty of this place, a kind of womb of light. Though many tourists were there, most of us seemed to understand that these spaces were cathedrals of a sort, and required silence of those who entered, so the vision of the rupas could enter us fully, and we could begin to lose our familiar orientation to our own identities, and become Buddha ourselves.

I still look at those photographs that I took that day. I cannot even imagine who the person was who sidled up to a Buddha statue so much larger than herself and got silent permission to let her eyes rest on this venerated being.

And river and tradition continue: the mother Mekong, glittering Luang Prabang, and mysterious Pak Ou. All three are gateless gates. One must pass through and beyond outer appearances to the inner and more subtle world of who we really are, which is reflected in those soaring roofs, the gold and stillness of the temples, in the wildness, dirt and decay, coffee and croissants, hustlers and weavers of the city; and the flow and drift of the river, this great river that is always changing, giving life and taking it away, and back again to the temples that reflect light and hold shadows faithfully so we can cool our striving. That is what the light of the Buddha reveals to us: the truth of impermanence, the possibility of transcendence. This, I believe, is what can be found by looking within and looking through the eyes of Luang Prabang, and the eyes of this marvelous book.

Roshi Joan Halifax, Ph.D, is a Buddhist teacher, Zen priest, and anthropologist. She is the author of *Standing at the Edge: Finding Freedom Where Fear and Courage Meet*, and *Being with Dying*. She is the founder, abbot, and head teacher of Upaya Institute and Zen Center in Santa Fe, New Mexico.

Sunset over
the Mekong

In the Buddha's Light

JOANNA HURLEY

THE SOUND OF A FAMILIAR SONG GONE AWRY pulled me out of a deep sleep. The blend of voices was peculiar, and the effort to figure out why spiraled my mind into consciousness. It sounded like Madonna in a medley with James Taylor, but even in my groggy state, I couldn't imagine those two singing together. Where was I that this could be happening? I rolled over, got out of bed, and found myself face-to-face with a wad of mosquito netting. Quickly untangling myself, I propped myself up on my elbows and looked around. As my eyes adjusted to the dawn light, I could make out dark teak louvers shading the doors just beyond the bed. I stood up, stumbled and nearly slid across the polished wood floor, and stepped out onto the balcony.

The morning mist hovered like a veil. As I watched, it slowly lifted, and the Mekong River, one of the mightiest and longest in all of Asia, revealed itself in pastel waves of blue and green just a few hundred yards away. I looked down, and saw a garden thick with bright green palm trees and orange, pink, and purple birds of paradise and heliconia plants rising like abstract parrots out of the brume. I turned around, and was dazzled by the glittering splendor of Luang Prabang, the spires of its golden temples piercing the sky.

I had never thought to go there until my friend, the photographer Jack Parsons, suggested we undertake a project on the temples and culture of this enchanting, small city of about 30,000 people, which is one of the most historic in Southeast Asia. He and his wife, Becky, had visited some years earlier, and fallen in love with it. I had been captivated by the stories he had told and pictures he had shown me upon their return. Although I had written some journalistic pieces over the years, as a longtime publicist and book packager I hadn't written anything more complex than a press release for some time. I was intrigued by the opportunity to flex my muscles as an essayist, and by the idea of spending time in a place about which I knew virtually nothing, on a continent that I had never visited, with someone with whom I had long enjoyed working and whose photography I admired.

Jack suggested we stay there for a month, which suited me just fine. I am the kind of traveler who prefers to stay in one place for a while to let it soak in, to get a sense of the land and the people. My last long trip to an area of the world that was as unfamiliar to me had been to Venezuela to climb a *tepui* in the southeastern part of the country, so I jumped at the chance.

With over sixty-five wats (temples) and a perfectly preserved royal palace, Luang Prabang, the former capital of the Lao kingdom for over seven hundred years, is one of the most historic cities in southeast Asia, thanks to a 1995 UNESCO World Heritage Site designation and the assiduous efforts of its communist leaders to keep it that way.

It was not always so. When the Pathet Lao toppled the royal Lao government in 1975, their rule was harsh, and tens of thousands fled the country, including many monks and intelligentsia. This exodus left it deprived of some of its most talented individuals, as well as the leaders of the Buddhist community. In the mid-1980s, the leaders of the Lao PDR (People's Democratic Republic) realized they needed to open up the country in order to survive economically, so they hired foreigners to advise them on developing a tourism industry, and relaxed their stance on the practice of Buddhism.

Although Laos is emerging as a destination for American tourists, Thailand and Vietnam, with their miles of coastline and more developed urban areas, are much more popular. But word is definitely out amongst Europeans and Australians, and the neighboring Chinese, who flood the city for two weeks around Chinese New Year, which falls anywhere from late January through mid-February in the Gregorian calendar. In central Luang Prabang, almost every other private home is turned into a guesthouse, and a huge night market with wares from all over the country as well as from China, Vietnam, and Thailand caters to the seemingly endless supply of tourists. The Lao response to this massive influx is an attitude of "*bo bpen nyang*" (loosely translated as "*c'est la vie*" or "*whatever*"), while also trying to benefit economically however they can.

Luang Prabang is situated at the confluence of two rivers, the Mekong and the Nam Khan. On a map the older part of the city looks like the thumb of a right hand on its side pointing northeast, with the newer part of town and the airport (on the other side of the Nam Khan) occupying the area between the thumb and forefinger. Except for the area around Luang Prabang, where the river snakes inland and east and then back west for a few dozen miles, the Mekong comprises most of Laos's border with Thailand, which is why it was relatively easy for refugees and dissidents to flee there when the Pathet Lao took over the country. Laos shares its northern border with China and Myanmar, its eastern with Vietnam, and southern with Cambodia.

Perhaps Laos's location in the midst of all these countries accounts for the remarkably mellow attitude of its citizens, who at various times have been under the rule of most of their neighbors or their ancestors. These include the ancient Khmer, who migrated from the north about 3,000 years ago and ended up settling primarily in what is now Cambodia; the Tai people, who migrated from Yunnan province in China in the 10th century throughout what is now Southeast Asia; as well as more recently the French, from the end of the 1800s until their retreat in 1945.

But after spending a month in and around Luang Prabang, I concluded that the main reason for the Lao laissez-faire mindset is their unshakable devotion to

Outskirts of Ban Na Nyang

Buddhism, which is the predominant religion, and, more than that, a way of life for most Lao. Despite the fact that the United States dropped more than 2 million tons of ordnance on Laos during the Vietnam War—making Laos the most-bombed per capita country in history— during my stay I only met one person who mentioned the war.

He was a handsome, wiry, older man with a quick gait who fell into step with us one afternoon as we were walking on a dirt path above a small village on the other side of the Mekong. In broken English, he asked us if we were American. When we said yes, he told us he had lived in the north during the war, in the now-famous caves near Sam Neua. While he didn't explicitly say (and we didn't ask), from that we deduced that it was likely he had been in the army of the Pathet Lao who, as communists, were closely aligned with the Vietnamese communists. And he looked to be about the right age. When the U.S. started bombing Laos, the Pathet Lao built a virtual city inside those caves, complete with hospitals, schools, markets, and military barracks that hid some 20,000 people for nine years between 1964 and 1973. We were quick to let him know that neither one of us had been in or approved of the war. Jack was too old to have been drafted; I was a child and then a teenager at the time. When we told him that we were deeply ashamed of what our government had done to Laos and the Lao people, he slowly nodded, looking at us thoughtfully with what seemed like a kind of bittersweet satisfaction.

The long flight over the Pacific was pretty much like any other long flight I had taken, but the extreme courtesy of the Thai Air flight attendants and their beautiful dresses, as colorful as East Indian saris but more form-fitting, reminded me that I was en route to Asia. Standing in the security line snaking through Bangkok's Suvarnabhumi Airport, I was excited to see people of many more ethnicities than I was used to encountering even in the multicultural United States, South America, or Western Europe. Varied as they were, most were Asian, from the "stan" countries of Central Asia as well as from Mongolia, China, Japan, Thailand, Laos, Vietnam, and Singapore. With our white skin and blue eyes, Jack and I were definitely in the minority. Slowly the disconcerting realization took hold that, unlike everywhere else I had traveled, here I was not going to be able to pass for a local.

Once in the air again, I looked out the window in anticipation. All I could see of Bangkok were the runways of the airport, the superhighways connecting it to the Oz-like city I could see shimmering faintly in the distance, and the same nondescript warehouse buildings that pimple the outskirts of European and American cities. Just before we headed high up into the clouds, I glimpsed rice paddies and bright green fields under cultivation by farmers bent over beneath conical bamboo hats. Then I knew I really was in Asia.

I didn't see much else until we started our descent into Luang Prabang, when the steeply rounded, lush mountains like those in Chinese brush paintings came into view, jutting like thumbs into the sky. I stared at them in amazement. I had always thought the rendering of the mountains in those paintings rather stylized. My profound ignorance about where I was going began to sink in.

When we arrived at the tiny airport in Luang Prabang, we were met by Kamphan, who was to be our landlord for the next month. We had been introduced to him through our friends Joanna (Jo) Smith and Veomanee (Veo) Douangdala, who run Ock Pop Tok ("East Meets West"), a weaving cooperative based in Luang Prabang that promotes and preserves Laos's rich textile and craft traditions. We had met them when they exhibited at the International Folk Art Market, which has been held annually since 2002 in Santa Fe, and for whose umbrella organization, the International Folk Art Alliance, I have worked over the years, first doing publicity and then producing a tenth anniversary book on the Market. Some of the images that Jack took on our trip are in that book.

Kamphan was a Lao man of medium height and build, in his mid-fifties, I guessed, with rectangular wire-rimmed glasses, straight, graying hair combed to the side, and a deeply-lined, long face that looked very serious until he smiled, and the wrinkles turned into laugh lines.

We bustled into a white mini-van and took off toward Luang Prabang down a two-lane road. Vans, small cars, motorbikes, and bicycles all steadily made their way in no particular lane, and with no particular haste, the effect being one of effortless flow as opposed to the chaos such a situation would create on a highway in the United States. Houses were sparse and the vegetation brown and spindly—not that much different from what lines the highways in the American Southwest or Midwest, except that bright green rice paddies tended by men and women in those unmistakably Asian conical hats were visible beyond. It was mid-afternoon and the sun was still high in the sky. I guessed the temperature to be about 80 degrees Fahrenheit and even more humid, and reveled in the sensation of moisture on my skin and hair, which felt really good after the high, dry air of Santa Fe.

As we got closer to the city itself, the sides of the two-lane road grew dense with houses and shops. Most were small cottages constructed of white-washed cement, brick, or wood, with pitched roofs of red tile, slatted wood, or thatch. At one point we rounded a corner and, at the T-stop, encountered a very long one-story white building with a shallow red-tile roof and an immaculate green lawn. The exterior was understated yet imposing, like that of a government building. I learned later that it had once been a hospital and was now an Amantaka Resort, part of one of the most elegant and expensive hotel chains in the world.

Minutes later, after having navigated a complex roundabout that seemed to channel all the traffic in the city, we arrived at our destination, a beautiful stucco and wood house on the corner of a short one-lane street and Souvanna Banlang,

Sakkarine Road

one of two main streets in the city that parallels the Mekong (the name changes to Souvanna Khamphong as it gets closer to the confluence of the Nam Khan and the Mekong). The other main street is Sisavangvong Avenue, named for the penultimate Lao king who ruled for more than fifty years until he died in 1959. Its name also changes, to Sakkarine Road, as it snakes northeast toward the rivers' junction. Sisavangvong's son, Savang Vatthana, was deposed by the Pathet Lao in 1975, and sent to a reeducation camp at Sam Neua. He is believed to have died there in 1984, a sad fate for someone who was by all accounts a gentle man, and a poet who wore the trappings of his royal status very lightly even before they lost their meaning.

Our house sat high on the street, just above the river. We entered through the back yard, past a red spirit house that sat atop a carved pedestal. It looked like a miniature temple with two steep roofs accented with gold paint and incense sticks, and fresh marigolds and candles strewn about its tiny courtyard. Spirit worship exists to some extent in most Southeast Asian Buddhist traditions, but the Lao believe especially in the energies, or *phi*, of places, including temples, homes, and land, and of plants, such as rice, that grow in a particular place. The *phi,* then, can be loosely understood as forces of nature. According to tradition, they must be honored with an offering of rice or fruit in the spirit house. Doing this on a regular basis is an important gesture of respect, as well as a request for protection.

The back gate of the house opened onto a long alleyway that provided a glimpse into the life of the neighborhood. It was also a shortcut to the center of town and the markets. Most people (including us) entered their homes through their alley gates, and often hung out there throughout the day and into the evening, chatting and cooking on small hibachi-type stoves. We greeted them several times a day as we passed with a cheerful "*sa bai dee!*" (hello), and received a friendly nod or "sa bai dee!" in return.

The only ones who didn't speak to us owned a small restaurant across the street on the Mekong where we went the first evening. They were really unfriendly and the service was terrible. We tried the place again and received the same treatment. So we dubbed them "the surly people." It got to the point where it was funny how rude they were. Their reaction was so conspicuously different from that of just about everyone else we met in Luang Prabang, we wondered what was up. We found out toward the end of our visit that the owner of our house had gotten it from their relative in payment for a debt, and they carried a grudge. Apparently they had not heard of the concept of *bo bpen nyang!*

Inside the house, the dark wood beams supporting the ceiling looked like the *vigas* in my house in Santa Fe, except that they were made of teak instead of pine. The walls were whitewashed stucco over concrete instead of plaster over adobe as at home, but the feeling was similar: cool, clean, and grounding. The flooring was wood in a few places, but mostly weathered red tile. The roof was teak, and pitched; the house had two stories. The living room opened onto a garden full of beautiful green ferns, snowy hibiscus with lime green centers, saffron and fuchsia canna plants, and milky-white plumeria (the national plant of Laos) with their bright pink centers and distinctive black outline on the petals.

Upstairs were two bedrooms, each with a bed shrouded in mosquito netting, an armoire, and long windows framed by dark teak, louvered shutters. I quickly got into the habit of opening them at night to let in the cool air, and closing them in the early morning to keep out the heat, as I do in the summer with my windows in Santa Fe. A covered wooden balcony wrapped around the south side of the second floor and afforded a view over the garden, the street, and the river beyond.

I would have liked to sit there meditating in the early morning, or watching the sun go down over the Mekong in the evening, but those were fantasies quickly dispelled. Tinny Asian pop music blared from the neighbors' radios starting at dawn, and didn't stop until the 11:30 pm curfew. (When I inquired as to the reason for the curfew, I was given reasons ranging from: "communism," or that people needed to get up early to give alms to the monks; more on that below.) After that jarring wake-up the first morning, I stopped trying to figure out who was singing and whether or not they were trying to imitate western musicians or just sounded that way, and took to sleeping with earplugs every night.

During the day, when we weren't out visiting temples or other sites, I spent most of my time in the house in the living room, relaxing on the simple platform sofas, reading, and listening to jazz on Jack's iPod, which effectively drowned out the annoying music from across the street, at least for a while. The bookshelves on the walls behind the sofas were lined with dozens of volumes in French and English on the art and history of Southeast Asia.

Over the weeks to come I would be grateful for that library, for it contained the best books I found on Lao culture either before or after my trip. The others were the mystery novels of the British writer Colin Cotterill, one of whose books Jack had given me to read on the plane. They feature the fictional Dr. Siri Paiboun, who is the sole national coroner in the mid-1970s, after the Pathet Lao have taken over the country. Dr. Siri is inhabited by the soul of a long-dead Hmong shaman whose supernatural "assistance" gets him into as many scrapes as out, but helps him solve the crimes. The novels are quirky and funny, and capture the spirit of the Lao people, their sardonic sense of humor, their great capacity for socializing and fun, and their absolute refusal to be dismayed or kept down by the powers-that-be, no matter how harsh or autocratic. *Bo bpen nyang.*

At the end of the day after visiting temples, Jack would have a beer and I a glass of wine, often with our guide, Nikhom, and Khong, our driver. We would sit in the living room with the doors open to the garden, and review the photos Jack had taken of the temples we had visited.

We found Nikhom, too, through Jo and Veo. Nikhom had recently gone out on his own after working with a travel agency. His English was less than perfect, but his personality, warm and ebullient, and his smile, like that of a Lao Cheshire cat, immediately won us over. He was barely into his thirties, with a young wife, a small child, and a furry, brown and white puppy that looked just like one of my beloved Australian sheepdogs at home. His wife was a seamstress, and they lived in a small house in a bustling village or *ban* on the outskirts of town.

Because he spoke no English, Khong was more of an enigma. We learned that he, too, was married, which surprised us. Khong seemed more like an Asian Tony Manero (John Travolta's character in *Saturday Night Fever*), an impression enhanced by the loud rock n' roll ring tone on his cell phone, and the way he swaggered when he walked, like he owned whatever place he happened to be. His smile was as broad and easy as Nikhom's, and he piloted his *tuk tuk* like a pro. A tuk tuk is a small pickup truck or motor bike retrofitted with the cab open to the back, where two wooden bench seats face each other under a plastic awning.

With Kong driving and Nikhom guiding us, Jack and I visited more than forty temples in and around Luang Prabang, most in the city itself, but also a few in outlying villages on the other side of the Mekong. We settled into a routine of visiting temples in the morning, breaking for lunch, and touring more wats in the afternoon.

No matter where we went, we found that even the smallest, simplest wats were lovingly and carefully maintained, clearly to the best of the abilities and resources of the people in their neighborhoods. The variety was enormous. Many in the city were huge, clustered in complexes with several buildings and dozens of monks, havens of tranquility in the midst of the bustle around them. Across the river we found others that were more like meditation chapels, tended only by two or three monks living in rustic huts on stilts at the edge of thick forest.

From the elegant to the humble, each was full of statues of Buddhas in all sizes fashioned from all kinds of materials: clay, amber, jade, silver, oxidized bronze, and gold. There was always one very large Buddha, sometimes on a dais, sitting at the back of the main room or *sim*, flanked by dozens of others, like a benign warrior spirit in the midst of his retinue. Candles surrounded and illuminated them, casting elongated shadows on the walls, which were often richly ornamented with painted scenes from the Jataka, the mythic stories of the 547 lives of the Buddha before he became enlightened. Offerings of yellow and orange marigolds, in vases or loose, covered the ground, or crowded the dais, or tables in front, along with a kind of ornament called *don po ngun po kham* ("tree of light silver" or "tree of gold") that looked like a tiny Christmas tree with pink and green lights strung on a spiraling metal scaffold. The bigger temples often had boomboxes, used to record and broadcast the monk's chanting. Even though the monks have sleeping quarters nearby, it's clear that the temple is their real home, the focus of their lives, and where they spend most of their time. When they tire after hours of meditation, they often simply lie down on the floor and fall asleep.

When I saw their rumpled blankets, which was often, I was tempted to touch them to see if they were still warm. The feeling was innocent and natural, underscoring the idea that the temple was home not just to the monks, but to anyone. I often saw homeless people seeking shelter, dogs sleeping on the altars, and sometimes even a cat curled into a reliquary.

Yet there is subtle protocol to respect when entering a wat (at least for humans). It is customary to remove one's shoes, and for women to cover their shoulders, although I saw many tourists who did not observe that rule. I quickly got over my initial resistance to being barefoot in a public place and came to love standing on the cool tile that covered the floor of many temples, or on the soft, dirt floors of the more rustic and remote wat*s*.

The first temple we went to was *Wat Xieng Thong*, located at the northeastern tip of the city where the Mekong meets the Nam Khan. It is widely acknowledged as the grandest of all the temples in Laos. Built in 1559 by King Settha-thirat, who ruled from 1548 to 1571, this temple earned Luang Prabang its UNESCO World Heritage Site designation in 1995. The complex is spectacular, huge and ornate, in architecture and setting, and in the variety and number of buildings. What initially struck me as garish was revealed upon closer inspection to be the product of delicate and painstaking artistry, and a kind of free-flowing yet very considered approach to design.

The walls, ceilings and part of the supporting mahogany struts and pilasters are drenched in gold leaf, and embellished with bright, almost neon-colored ceramic tiles. Hundreds of statues of Buddhas of all shapes and sizes crowd the dais and the floor surrounding it.

There are standing Buddhas carved out of emerald and lapis lazuli, seated Buddhas of bronze, green with age, and Buddhas of silver. There are tiny, amber Buddhas that fit into the palm of the hand like thick, shiny pennies, golden Buddhas, and five foot tall Buddhas sitting in the lotus position. Many of them are encrusted with glittering blood-red rubies, cobalt blue sapphires, and deep green emeralds. Light from the windows, from cracks in the roof, and from candles and incense placed on the altar and on the floor beyond bounces off the corners of the statues, illuminating the Buddhas and the little metal trees. The ceiling depicts scenes from heaven and hell painted in black and gold on water buffalo hide. It, too, gleams in the light, and figures from its tableaux loom large in the shadows and dance along the walls. The effect is dazzling.

Facing the temple outside, it appears that the roof is steeply slanted with a second, shorter roof covering the one beneath, topped by a stylized serpent or naga angling into the sky. Looking at it from the side, one can see that the temple is much larger than it appears from the front, and that there is actually a series of sweeping double roofs, four in all, each topped with its own naga. Nagas are snake deities, also often depicted as dragons, and feature prominently in both Hindu and Buddhist iconography.

The exterior back wall of the main temple features a gorgeous, elaborate mosaic of the Tree of Life made of turquoise, blue, purple, green, and silver glass tiles. It was added in 1960, at the behest of King Savang Vatthana. This motif, common to many religions, here symbolizes the link between heaven and Earth.

Next to the main temple is The Chapel of the Standing Buddha, which looks like a tiny reliquary or stupa, with whitewashed walls and a whitewashed base. Five steep steps are set into the base. A series of gold-sheathed landings above them leads to the entry, crowned with a richly carved, gilded pediment covered in glass mosaic with a lotus at the center.

My favorite building in the complex, indeed, of all that I saw in Luang Prabang, was La Chapelle Rouge (the Red Chapel), built in 1960, by the same craftsmen who created the Tree of Life mosaic. Small and exquisite as a Fabergé egg, it sits atop a turquoise-painted stone base that shimmers like a mirage of water in the desert. Walls of deep magenta plaster rise up from this tiny sea. They are embedded with millions of brightly colored glass tiles arranged in the shapes of people, animals, plants, and Buddhas enacting stories of heaven and Earth.

Above the walls, three steeply pitched teak roofs adorned with nagas stack one atop the other. Curved golden struts mimicking the sinewy tails of the nagas hold up the corners and sides. Voluptuous golden figures dance in stylized splendor on the doors, a reminder of the Indian origins of Buddhism. In the Indian tradition, whether Hindu, Jain, or Buddhist, the sensuous is seen as an integral part of the sacred.

Near La Chapelle Rouge is another similar building, smaller, with only two roofs. This is the library or *hor tai*, which houses ancient Buddhist manuscripts. It, too, is painted a rich reddish-pink, and its exterior is covered in an intricate mosaic of bright glass tiles. I marveled that venerated texts were stored in such a vibrant-looking place.

Many of the temples we visited had resident cats and dogs, often maimed in some way, for there is little veterinary care in this exceedingly poor country. All the dogs I saw were skinny, and short-haired, none much taller than my knees. Whenever I saw one, which was often, I was reminded of a conversation with a friend who opined that, left to their own devices without breeders and fancy food and comfortable living conditions, all dogs would eventually evolve into generic canines that would look like these or the "rez dogs" that are ubiquitous on the Native American reservations of the Southwest United States. Seeing these animals taking refuge in the temples without anyone shooing them out underscored for me the inclusiveness of the Buddhist philosophy and its reverence for all sentient beings.

In my attempt to understand the wats, and the culture that created them, my mind searched for comparisons that were familiar to me. I was reminded of the great European cathedrals and the vital role they played in their communities throughout the Middle Ages and the Renaissance. Large or small, humble or elaborate, the wats are often situated in the centers of their neighborhoods and, as the cathedrals once did, serve as refuges not just for the monks who tend them but for anyone, from any walk of life. Similarly, each community spends as much money as it can afford on its wat's upkeep, and local stonemasons, tile makers, artists, and craftspeople maintain them.

The larger wats contain even more ornamentation and gilt than the great cathedrals such as Chartres or Rennes, even when one considers how brilliant those cathedrals must have looked in their heyday. I found this phenomenon jarring at first, and it made me wonder (not for the first time) why almost all cultures, East and West, spend so much money on the outward manifestations of

Cat in reliquary,
Wat Xieng Mene

their religions, regardless of the poverty of the people. I've concluded that the human spirit needs something to be in awe of and honor, and a purpose greater than the quotidian to work toward.

Buddhism has several variants, Vajrayana, and Mahayana chief among them. The predominant strain in Laos is Theravada, a form of monastic Buddhism also referred to as "The School of the Elders" or "The Southern Tradition." This form of Buddhism is also practiced in Sri Lanka, from which it spread to Thailand, Vietnam, and Burma. It is thought that Theravada was introduced to Laos by the Mon people, who came from Thailand sometime after the sixth century A.D. The Mon were followed by the Tai people, who originated in China, and migrated south in the tenth century into present-day Myanmar, Thailand, Laos, and Vietnam. The names of over a dozen Lao ethnic groups begin with the prefix "Tai," attesting to their strong and enduring influence.

One of the reasons Buddhism spread so successfully throughout Asia was its malleability: Its proponents had no problem adapting it to local culture and existing religious practices. In Laos, for example, Buddhist proselytizers wholeheartedly embraced and incorporated the ancient tradition of spirit cults, which also has persisted in northeastern Thailand into the twenty-first century despite the efforts first of indigenous kings, then the French, and more recently, the Pathet Lao, to eliminate it.

Another distinguishing feature of Lao Buddhism is the fact that many young men, especially those raised in cities, spend several months to several years as novice monks in a monastery, where they receive their education. They learn to read and write and about the major tenets of Buddhism and the Buddhist way of life. Some of the monks we met in the larger monasteries were studying English as well. This option is not open to girls. While there are occasionally nuns associated with some of the temples—more as servants than anything else, it seems, as they clean the monk's quarters and wash their robes—there appears to be no place for women within the hierarchy of Lao Buddhism. However, there are girls in the elementary school in Luang Prabang, which may be one of the achievements of the communist regime.

Regardless of their limited access to formal education, women play an important role in maintaining Lao cultural traditions, especially weaving, which is a source of great pride as well as income for many families. Before we arrived in Luang Prabang, Ock Pop Tok had launched a new project in a village of the Tai Lue ethnic group that was located a couple hours' drive north of the city. We rode up there one day with Jo and a couple other women who weave with the cooperative to observe a meeting of the Tai Lue women with their counterparts who were members of a Tai Dam community from Phongsaly province, which is in the far north of Laos. The Tai Lue women were explaining to the Tai Dam women how working with Ock Pop Tok allowed them to revitalize their weaving traditions and create a sustainable business model that generated income for their community. Even though we could not understand one word of what was said, we could feel the tension and urgency in the air, as the Tai Dam were also considering an offer from a Chinese company to grow rubber trees on the same land where, for centuries, they had been cultivating cotton plants and the mulberry trees on whose leaves silkworms thrive. The land could not sustain cotton, mulberry *and* rubber trees, so it was an either-or deal. The lure was the immediate cash the village would receive from allowing the Chinese to plant the rubber trees.

But rubber trees take ten years to mature. By that time the Tai Dam would have long since spent the money, and be left with fallow fields and no sustainable livelihood. This is, unfortunately, a scenario that is all too common throughout the developing world: quick profit vs. economic, cultural, and environmental sustainability. But to a tiny, poor community like that of the Tai Dam, the promise of immediate cash was nearly irresistible. This was a pivotal meeting that would in large part determine its future. And the women were running the show.

Ban Nan Nyong

The Tai Dam women arrived, dressed in their finest silk blouses and *sinhs* or skirts made of a rectangular piece of multi-colored woven cotton fabric that is wrapped around the wearer's body and held in place at the waist with a silver or cloth belt. Their glistening black hair was beautifully coiled on top of their heads and fastened with ornamental lacquered chopsticks, many with silver tips. Lao women typically wear elaborately worked and chiseled silver jewelry, and the Tai Dam women were wearing lots of it, bangles, earrings, and necklaces. They overwhelmed the Tai Lue women, who were dressed in short cotton trousers and blouses, little or no jewelry, their hair pulled back into simple ponytails. Interestingly, to us outsiders, it looked like the Tai Dam were thriving while the Tai Lue were not, but the opposite was the case.

We took our places at the back of the large room, which we gathered was a kind of ceremonial and entertaining space. It was on the second floor of a large wooden, pitched-roof house set into the ground on stilts, and accessible via a wooden ladder. Although none of what was said was comprehensible to us, it was clear from the body language and from the laughter and cordiality that was much in evidence by the meeting's end that the consensus was moving in the direction of working with Ock Pop Tok. We learned later (with some relief) from Jo that the Tai Dam had joined their Village Weavers project. The products made with their cloth are now featured on the Ock Pop Tok website, along with those from twelve similar projects in various villages throughout Laos.

Laos is a country of diverse ethnic groups—from twenty-nine to sixty seven, depending on the source one consults, each with its own distinct culture, dress, and dialect. In the same way, Luang Prabang is a collection of *bans* or villages, each with its own temple, the focus of the community. The city is a study in contrasts, but nothing is hard-edged. Young monks in centuries-old temples broadcast their chanting on sound systems for the whole neighborhood to hear; young women and men living in villages without modern plumbing commute into town on motorbikes, wearing crash helmets. Cell phones are ubiquitous.

Luang Prabang is famous for its morning rite of giving alms to the monks. Shortly before dawn, their hands full of rice balls, fruit, and other simple delicacies, people line Sisavangvong Avenue to await the monks, who emerge from their temples to receive the flowers and food. Tourists can participate, but we were warned to be quiet and reverent, to keep our eyes downcast, and to kneel if possible, to show respect.

On the morning we went, I found myself in front of the Luang Prabang secondary school, among laughing boys (and girls, I was pleased to see) in white and maroon uniforms. Jack stood on the other side of the street where there were fewer people, so as to get better shots of the procession and the onlookers. A tiny old lady in worn, baggy stretch pants and a red cotton top stood to my left with her little granddaughter, who wore a blue and yellow shift. As we smiled at each other and settled in to await the arrival of the monks, a group of fancy-looking tourists—from the Amantaka , I guessed—piled out of a sleek, white van and commandeered a chunk of the sidewalk in front of us.

They wore expensive-looking silk jackets and held rice balls that their guide handed them from a lacquered wooden case. Another man raised umbrellas to shield them from the sun (which was not all that high or hot at 6:00 AM), and a third set up stools for them to sit on. Even though they were inches away from me, neither they nor their handlers made eye contact or apologized for pushing in front of us. *Bo bpen nyang.*

Cozy in my fleece pullover, I pondered what I would do if any monks who looked like abbots passed by. Nikhom had warned me on our first day visiting temples that I must quickly "get small" (he didn't say how) if I encountered an abbot, and not look him in the eye, as that would be disrespectful from a woman. At 5'7" I am slightly taller than the average American woman, and definitely taller than most Lao. As luck would have it, on that cool morning giving alms, I saw no abbots, only young monks my height or shorter, most of them staring straight ahead with serious expressions. Even though the monks rarely made eye contact with me, there was a kind of intimacy to the ritual that was more satisfying to me than dropping a coin or dollar into the collection plate in the Roman Catholic churches of my youth.

After giving alms and having breakfast at a nearby café, we hopped back into our tuk-tuk, piloted by the ever-cheerful and capable Khong, and headed for the morning market about a mile down the street. The market, called Pho-Si, sits more or less across from Wat Phousi, and spreads over several of the side streets that link Sisavangvong Avenue with Souvanna Khamphong. Imagine rickety wooden stalls with vendors selling everything from nail polish to fish, fried rice, fresh coriander, ginger root, bamboo sprouts, and exotic fruits like the pink-snouted dragon fruit named for its yellow and green spikes.

There were also familiar fruits like red grapes, green apples, juicy mangos, and the wonderful, mini bananas that I had loved to eat in South America, and other exotics like longan, which looks something like a giant kiwi fruit but is more oval in shape, and durian, which has a bright green husk covered in fleshy pink thorns. I closed my eyes and inhaled the pungent smell of fish mixed with the piquant, sweet scents of the fruits and the fragrant perfume of the coriander. It felt so sensual, exotic, and otherworldly. For a moment I was a child lost in an Asian fairytale.

Another day we went to the spectacular Pak Ou Caves, which are located in limestone cliffs about sixteen miles up and across the river from Luang Prabang and considered one of the most sacred sites in Laos. To get there, we went down to the river where Nikhom hailed a boatman and negotiated a price. We jumped in, leaving Kong with his tuk tuk to await our return. The boat was a type of pirogue that looked like a cross between a gondola and a canoe, low-slung in the water, with a blue hull and a motor at the stern. The boatman stood up as he plied the waters, and sat when he turned on the motor, which he did when the current was slow. He wore a faded cap, an even more faded t-shirt, and long, raggedy shorts. He rarely spoke, just squinted and stared at the river.

There are two caves at Pak Ou, the upper, which is called Tham Theung, and Tham Ting, the lower. They contain thousands of statues of the Buddha placed there by pilgrims over many centuries. As in the temples, the effect is breathtaking, but more subtle: As one walks into the caves and the eyes adjust to the low light, the Buddhas look ghostly, the shadows of even the tiniest magnified by the light of hundreds of burning votive candles. Everywhere I looked there were Buddhas, on the rocky outcroppings at waist-height and above, on the dirt at my feet underneath the ledges, in clusters like small armies at the back of the caves. As I walked through with dozens of people talking softly, their voices echoing in a kind of ethereal surround-sound, I couldn't decide if I was in a museum or at a requiem.

After several hours in the cool darkness of the caves, I was happy to re-board our boat, hear the water lapping the sides, and feel the breeze on my face. On the ride home, we asked Nikhom about his life. He told us that, like many young men in Laos, he had received his education as a novice monk. But unlike most of them, he spent four years in the temple; the average is two. He considered staying longer, but left because earthly delights called to him: He wanted a wife and a family.

We later met his cousin, who was one of the most cultured and refined men I have ever encountered. Taller than most Lao, with jet-black, wavy hair, an aquiline nose, sloping forehead and slightly upturned chin, he emanated natural authority and grace. He spoke English with a posh British accent, which he told me he had acquired watching the BBC. He had spent nearly twenty years in one of the most revered wats in Luang Prabang, but ultimately left because his teacher told him he should pursue a "regular life." For a man like him, it is probably the greater challenge—and Buddhism is, after all, about spiritual evolution. He now runs a travel agency in Luang Prabang, and is married with children. But when he speaks of his life in the temple, his eyes and voice soften, revealing his longing for the past.

As I look again and again at Jack's photographs of the temples and their environs, their interiors and exteriors, the monk's quarters and the monks themselves, I am reminded of the gentleness of both Lao and Buddhist culture, and of their devotion to what to is essential: community and history, which both mirror and define our relationship to ourselves and our natures as human beings. There is a kind of purity in approaching life in that way that we in the United States seem largely to have lost; we glorify it in traditional cultures when we encounter them as tourists, and return home hungry for that timelessness and connection. Buddhism is about living in the moment—not the ephemeral moment of Instagram, Twitter, and Facebook—but the pure moment without our ego's involvement with it. It's the difference between shallowness and reverence, between having an attention span of eight seconds, and being in a calm, suspended state where we are unaware of time.

These pictures are like the wats themselves, blending awe for their sheer beauty that honors the forces that are greater than ourselves with the color and story that are integral to the life that bustles within and around the temples. There is a sense of peace in every one of these pictures that mirrors the still point of connection with all-that-is, that perfect emptiness that one strives to reach in meditation and rarely does, but whose impression is deep and lasting, even if the experience is momentary. *Bo bpen nyang.*

Author's note:

The Lao people refer to themselves and their country as "Lao;" hence the word is both a proper noun and an adjective. The "s" was added by the French to ease pronunciation, and it has stuck. Throughout this essay I have used the word "Laos" as the noun to refer to the country and "Lao" as an adjective for the people and their customs, although native Lao tend to use the word "lao" for both. Some English speakers, wanting to avoid colonial overtones, refer to the country as *Lao*, not *Laos*, but others, including some native Lao, believe use of the term that way by foreigners is pretentious. For an excellent discussion of the two terms and their relative merits, I recommend a short essay by Nick Enfield, a scholar at the Max Planck Institute of Psycholinguistics, with thanks to William deBuys for directing me to it. Enfield's piece originally appeared in the *Vientiane Times* in 1998, and can be accessed at http://laobumpkin.blogspot.com/2008/07/of-laos-and-laotians.html.

Rather than describe every temple we visited, I have chosen to focus on a few that made a particular impression on me. I don't pretend to be an historian, much less an architectural historian or religious scholar, so for those wishing more detailed information I have provided a short bibliography. I especially recommend Denise Heywood's *Ancient Luang Prabang*, which provides a brief history, and describes some thirty-four temples, as well as other significant buildings in and around Luang Prabang. William Dalrymple's excellent article (cited below) on the Ajanta Caves in India also provides a number of sources that will be helpful to those interested in more information on the origins and history of Buddhism.

Selected Bibliography

Cotterill, Colin. *Slash and Burn: A Dr. Siri Mystery Set in Laos.* New York: Soho Press, 2011.

________, *Love Songs from a Shallow Grave: A Dr. Siri Mystery Set in Laos.* New York: Soho Press, 2011.

________, *The Merry Misogynist.* New York: Soho Press, 2010.

________, *Anarchy and Old Dogs.* New York: Soho Press, 2008.

________,*Disco for the Departed*. New York: Soho Press, 2007.

________, *Thirty-Three Teeth.* New York: Soho Press, 2006.

________, *The Coroner's Lunch.* New York: Soho Press, 2005.

Cummings, Joe. Photography by Bill Wassman. *Buddhist Stupas in Asia: The Shape of Perfection.* Footscray, Victoria, Australia: Lonely Planet, 2002.

Dakin, Brett. *Another Quiet American: Stories of Life in Laos*. Bangkok: Asia Books, 2003.

Dalrymple, William, "The Greatest Ancient Picture Gallery," *The New York Review of Books*, October 23, 2014.

Evans, Grant. *A Short History of Laos, The Land in Between.* Crows Nest, New South Wales, Australia: Allen & Unwin, 2002.

Heywood, Denise. *Ancient Luang Prabang.* Bangkok: River Books, 2006.

Holt, John Clifford. *Spirits of the Place: Buddhism and Lao Religious Culture.* Honolulu: University of Hawai'i Press, 2009.

http://www.legaciesofwar.org

http://www.ockpoptok.com

Stuart-Fox, Martin. Photography by Steve Northrup. *Naga Cities of the Mekong: A guide to the temples, legends, and history of Laos.* Singapore: Media Masters, Ltd., 2006.

Zurick, David. *The Himalaya: Encounters with the Roof of the World.* Chicago: The Center for American Places at Columbia College, 2011.

Novice monk,
Wat Kok Pap

Interior,
Wat That Noi

Jade Buddha,
Wat Mai

Interior, Wat Xien Thong
(opposite) Interior detail, Wat Pa Huak

View through a window, Wat Xien Thong
(opposite) Front, Wat Xien Thong

Wat
Phouk Way

Nagas flanking
stairs, Wat Nong

Detail, nagas, Wat Xieng Thong
(opposite) Wat Sene

Roof, Wat Phouk Way
(opposite) Roof, Wat Mai

Wat Pa Phai

Monks preparing for a
celebration, Wat Monorom

Monk studying, Wat Phone Say

(opposite, top) Monk reading, Wat Meunna
(opposite, bottom) Chalkboard, Wat Ban Ou

Young monks, Wat Kok Pap

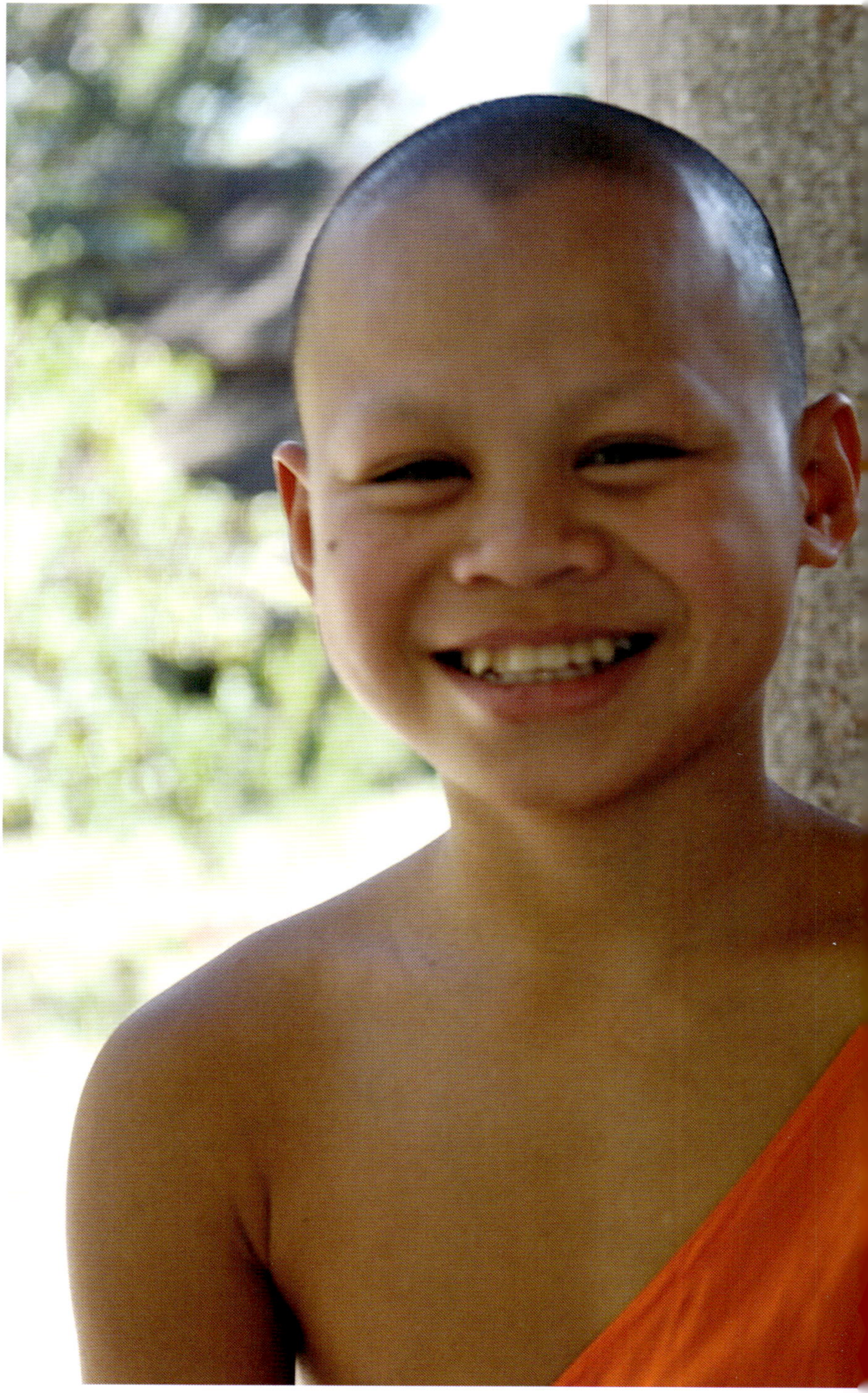

Monks reading outside Wat Meunna
(opposite) Older monk, Wat Pha Ya Thup

(left) *Don po ngun po kham,* “trees of silver or gold” with Buddha at Wat Ban Ou
(right) Interior, Wat Tao Hai
(opposite) Interior, Wat Meunna

Wat Monoram

Interior,
Wat Visoun

Monks sleeping
on the floor of
Wat Sakam

Interior, Wat Meunna

Wat Hosian

Door,
Wat Pha Ya Thup

Buddhas, Wat Mai

(following spreads)
Wat That Luang
with stupa
Wat That Noi with stupa

People and shoes
outside Wat Phon Sang

(opposte) Door,
Wat Xiene Mene

Interior, Wat Xiene

Monks at Wat Meunna complex

Buddhas, Wat Visoun
(opposite) Altar, Wat Xieng Thong

Interior, Wat Kok Pap

Portico, Wat Long Khoun

Roof, Wat Nong

(opposite) Exterior, Wat Moung Koie

Monk with Buddha, Wat Xieng Moun
(opposite) Monk praying outside Wat Khili
(following spread) Monks on morning alms walk, Sisavangvong Avenue

For Rent

(top) Monk
with puppy,
Wat Haht Haen

(botom) Monks
outside Wat Kok Pap

Monks doing chores
at Wat Tao Hai

Wat Kok Pap

Interior, Wat Chom Phet

Nagas lining staircase,
Wat Phousi

Gilded Buddhas,
Wat Phousi

Buddhas at entrance to Pak Ou Caves

Woman lighting candle,
Pak Ou Caves

Armies of Buddhas,
Pak Ou Caves

Interior, Wat Mai

Interior, Wat Pa Huak

Interior, Wat Long Khoun

Abbot, Wat Pha Long

Older Monks, Wat Aphay

Monk in his quarters, Wat Tao Hai
(opposite) Young monk in his quarters, Wat Sakam

Monk walking outside Wat Khili
(opposite) Exterior, Wat Long Khoun

Stupa at Wat Visoun
(opposite) Exterior, Wat Pha Ya Thup

Exterior, Wat Ban Tat Paene

Exterior, Wat Long Khoun

Monk and dogs,
Wat Pa Khe

Monk with cats,
Wat Xieng Thong

Monks bathing

Acknowledgments

THIS BOOK WOULD NOT BE POSSIBLE without the support of many people. First and foremost we would like to thank Veomanee Douangdala and Joanna Smith of Ock Pop Tok, the internationally recognized, Luang Prabang-based, artisan-social enterprise (www.ockpoptok.com) whose help was invaluable in planning our trip and introducing us to the people on the ground who made it happen. Some of them include our driver, Kong, and our guide, Nikhom, who were our invaluable daily companions; Nikhom's cousin Khansouk, a travel agent and former monk who explained to us the intricacies of a monk's apprenticeship; Khamphan Inthavong, the landlord of the beautiful house we rented; Richard Hsu, graphic designer and entrepreneur; Boun Khang Khuttao, former Deputy Director, Luang Prabang Provincial Department of Information, Culture, and Tourism; Veo's husband, Stephen Schipani, and Thongkhoun Soutthivilay, co-founder and co-director of the Traditional Arts and Ethnology Centre with whom we spent many enjoyable hours along with Veo and Jo. And of course all the monks and abbots who graciously allowed us into their temples and living quarters.

Closer to home we are most grateful to William deBuys, Sally Denton, and Debra Hughes for reading early drafts of the text; to Roshi Joan Halifax for providing the lovely preface; David Skolkin for the beautiful book design; Stuart Ashman and the International Folk Art Market for enthusiastically publishing the book; and Royden Muranaka, former sales director of the University of Hawai'i Press, and the rest of the team there for helping us put it out into the world.

About the Authors

Roshi Joan Halifax, Ph.D, is a Buddhist teacher, Zen priest, and anthropologist. Her most recent book is *Standing at the Edge: Finding Freedom Where Fear and Courage Meet* (Flatiron Books). She is the founder, abbot, and head teacher of Upaya Institute and Zen Center in Santa Fe, New Mexico. https://www.upaya.org

Joanna Hurley has spent her career in book publishing. An award-winning publicist, she is also co-founder of Radius Books, and former board chair of CENTER, a not-for-profit organization that honors and supports gifted and committed photographers. She is currently an agent/producer of fine art and photography books based in Santa Fe, New Mexico. www.hurleymedia.com

Award-winning photographer **Jack Parsons** is most famous for his elegant book photography that captures the visual heritage of the American Southwest. He has published seventeen books, including the iconic *Santa Fe Style* (Rizzoli), with Christine Mather and Sharon Woods, and *Lone Star Living* (Bulfinch Press), with the late Tyler Beard. www.jackparsonsdigital.com

(opposite) Detail, decorative panel,
Wat Xieng Thong

Publisher: International Folk Art Market
Distributor: University of Hawai'i Press
Project Coordinator & Editor: Joanna Hurley, HurleyMedia, LLC
Design & Production Director: David Skolkin

Published in 2020, First hardcover edition.

ISBN: 978-0-9891992-2-3

Printed in Singapore on acid-free paper.

The Library of Congress Pre-assigned Control number is available upon request.